THE SCORPION'S
QUESTION MARK

THE SCORPION'S
QUESTION MARK

J.D. DEBRIS

AUTUMN
HOUSE PRESS

pittsburgh

Cover Art by © Lou Jones / mptvimages.com
Book Design by Chiquita Babb
Author Photo by Karisma Price

Library of Congress Cataloging-in-Publication Data

Names: Debris, J. D., author.
Title: The scorpion's question mark / J.D. Debris.
Other titles: Scorpion's question mark (Compilation)
Description: Pittsburgh : Autumn House Press, [2023]
Identifiers: LCCN 2022053200 (print) | LCCN 2022053201 (ebook) | ISBN
  9781637680667 (paperback) | ISBN 9781637680674 (epub)
Subjects: LCGFT: Poetry.
Classification: LCC PS3604.E2365 S36 2023 (print) | LCC PS3604.E2365
  (ebook) | DDC 811/.6--dc23/eng/20221121
LC record available at https://lccn.loc.gov/2022053200
LC ebook record available at https://lccn.loc.gov/2022053201

Autumn House Press is a nonprofit corporation whose mission is the publication and
promotion of poetry and other fine literature. The press gratefully acknowledges
support from individual donors, public and private foundations, and government

 agencies. This book was supported, in part,
by the Greater Pittsburgh Arts Council
through its Allegheny Arts Revival Grant
and the Pennsylvania Council on the Arts, a
state agency funded by the Commonwealth
of Pennsylvania.

 This project is supported in part by the
National Endowment for the Arts. To find
out more about how National Endowment
for the Arts grants impact individuals and
communities, visit www.arts.gov.

CONTENTS

I

II
CHALINO SÁNCHEZ: A SEQUENCE

III

?

IV

GATO BARBIERI: A SEQUENCE

For Yusef Komunyakaa and J. D. Scrimgeour:
two generations of guidance.

Thank you, Jesus, for blindness that every once in
a great while allows one of us to hit the target.

— *John Edgar Wideman*

The game of doubting itself presupposes certainty.

—*Ludwig Wittgenstein*

I

APARECIDA, EARLY SPRING

A long exhale at the end
of a hyperventilating season.

All winter nothing touched
my neck except the clenched,

manic teeth of the electric razor,
the beachwind's salt. Marvin Hagler,

my home state's fiercest fighter,
a man so mean they say hair

feared his sweat-gleamed skull,
is gone. I've mimicked his ritual:

mornings, breathless, sprinting the hill.
A sea & continent apart, your curls

are on my mind. By the logic
& legend of that bald, fallen

boxer, your curls mean mercy,
are wild & fertile

as these blossoms blindsiding
New England spring—vines

around a cello's neck, its body split,
a beehive inside. I dreamt we kissed

so slow it was like breathing
for the first time.

THE VOICE OF HERCULES

Remembering that heavyweight
we'd call Hercules,
a mellow steroid fiend
who never sparred, just raised

barbells till he was swollen as that solemn
British killer from *Ninja II: Shadow
of a Tear*. He'd flex, hit vacuum
poses in ringside mirrors, taking photo

after photo, & lounge in the locker room,
nothing but a sideways Sox hat on.
A garden-variety goon
with a garbled, guttural monotone

& shriveled steroid balls:
so Hercules seemed, on the surface.
But every word he spoke was praise—
"So sick, bro"—softly, near inaudible.

One night, the gym screened a pay-
per-view—De La Hoya or Money May.
All us gym rats came back
in jewelry, jeans, & the reek

of cologne instead of sweat
to cozy up between dormant
heavy bags & watch the fights
projected on industrial concrete.

I brought my old acoustic
for between-fight amusement,
background-strumming a soundtrack
to our cacophony. Hercules sat

beside me, saying, "Bro,
can you play a corrido beat?"
I started to strum a stock waltz-meter,
& Hercules, in a bass bel canto

that could rumble the cheap seats
of an opera hall, began a Spanish ballad
about a lost bantamweight
named Amen, who had disappeared,

the lyrics went, to Mexico last spring,
whom no one had heard from since.
The gym was quiet one verse in.
Pay-per-view muted, everyone listening

to this supposed bonehead
channel beauty. To his ballad,
its fragility—"Fly,
little dove, fly," he'd sigh

at verses' end. I'm amazed
that no one laughed at him—
insults, back then, our lingua
franca & form of praise—

in that moment so holy
& ridiculous, when his lips formed Os
on long, pure
tones, & every chord

perfectly—somehow—
harmonized.
I can't tell you which prize-
fighter won that bout,

or if we gorged on pizza & beer,
blowing off our weight-making regimens.
I can't tell you if it rained, I can't pretend
to know if sparks flew inside all those ears

bent in unison toward the amen
Hercules incanted. As for him,
his trainer, a hard-ass marine,
got sick of his preening

& told him go find another gym
where he could kiss his biceps
in the mirror & drink his creatine
& beast his endless deadlift reps.

How many songs has he sung since,
in the shower of a distant gym
where he still takes his sweet time
soaping every ropelike vein?

What I know, I'll tell:
Around the campfire of the muted fights
that night, he was our horn of Gabriel,
our nightingale mid-flight.

Sing it again, Hercules?
                              "Aight."

ON THE BEACH AT NIGHT WITH PETE

A curled ribbon of carcinogens trails your finger
as we listen to a sermon from your phone,
feet on the picnic bench like we're still delinquents.
Your hunting dog's at ease. The beach is closed.

Your smoke swirls like a haunted chapel's incense,
& when the preacher pleads toward the stratosphere,
you punctuate the air with your American Spirit
like you hold the world's lightest hammer

& the night needs repair. We walked here
on the wet sand path behind the leftfield fence,
past darkened fishermen's houses on the harbor,
no whisper but that bare, buzzing fluorescence

above the docks. I smelled the bitter salt of lobster
traps, saw the marsh where midnight hung her curtains,
& whistled a couple bars of "Fisherman," the Congos'
call & response: hey brother Peter, hey brother John—

your name & mine soaked in another era's echo
& electricity, slow dub on a distant waterfront.
There was a decade when we thought we'd lost you
to bad transcendence & whatever contraband

your lungs could hold. That decade's done.
Let's start off with this dark: a silent diamond
with the chime of baseball bat aluminum
inside it, this dark with the distant hum of grinders

& lathes inside it. This dark that could swallow
sixty-hour workweeks & heavy machines,
your metal-splintered palms. This dark that palled
a decade. That, by your lighter's brief fire, gleams.

DRUNK WITH THE MERMAID

"The bottom of the sea is less cruel than you'd think,"
she tells me, four drinks deep at The Schooner Hannah
(the dive bar, not the boat), leaning in to play with the links

of my secondhand crucifix. She's the great-great-grand-
daughter of shipwrecked Cape Verdean whalers
who didn't drown, somehow, but instead built, from wet sand,

tidewrack, driftwood & clamshell, houses at the sea's nadir.
They fell for subaquatic fiancées & interbred, she tells me,
making a life in which they were the Ishmaels, the narrators,

not the interchangeable extras x-ed out of early
Melville revisions. She sounds like distant windchimes
when she exhales, & what I thought were a few stray

curls are really cursive, f-shaped slits below her jawline.
Weirdly familial five drinks deep, I think of my sister,
who, though not half-amphibian, fish, or dolphin,

is half-Polish & can swim like a motherfucker.
Me, I just sink.
                    She parts the dive bar's beaded curtains,
leads me down cobblestone streets to the pier,

& swan-dives in the harvest moon's reflection, extending
stone-smooth, polished fingers through the glint.
The bottom of the sea is less cruel than you'd think.

BEACH ROSE

after Montale & Tupac

Bring her the beach rose so she knows
by heart the harsh & jagged places mercy grows,
so she hears its song of salt & dismal odds
burst out in thorn-green from between the rocks.

Soft things spring from hardness, symmetry from chaos.
So through broken bones of driftwood & a shroud
of bees it shows, clinging to bent & rusted bolts,
lacing thin, spiked limbs through bottle shards.

Bring her the pink, interlocking infinity that survives
where no vine should, on tidewrack & defiance
alone. Let a blossom meet your pocketknife—
bring her the beach rose unlikely as life.

BAD YEAR IN & OUT OF NEW YORK

for Janelle Tan

The other day I was about to punch a wall,
but then I realized João Gilberto's version
of "Trolley Song" was on. It's impossible,
or at the very least, patently absurd,
to punch a wall in the midst of "Trolley
Song," which, as its title suggests, is a song

about a trolley, & is impossibly spry—every
known species of jazz chord, plus a few plucked
from hypothetical spheres, rushing, in a blur,
past the ear's fogged windows. My fist is pocked
with fighter's scars which, by all means,
should've faded by now, but haven't; I'm tired

of rendering my life in cipher, by which I mean
a thing meant to be cracked, & tonight I realize
"Trolley Song," via João Gilberto's sighing strings
& larynx, is the most potent rhythm in existence,
enough to render all our shouldered damage laughable.
In the week & a half since I saw you last,

all I've done is slow "Trolley Song" to a crawl
in an attempt to capture its lightning flash
of joy inside my melancholy instrument, & break all
of summer's half-assed chastity vows with the bodega
owner's niece, who sketches, during slow shifts,
apple-tree branches growing from a woman's head.

Your confiding ear knows all too well it's been a year
of snapped wishbones on a bachelor's plate,
a pile of broken clocks into which I've read

expressions of indifference, orgasm, or animal fear,
though the only decent reading is this: Times have passed
& might, if we're lucky, pass again. So bless the smallest

of small absurdities that turn our pain ridiculous.
The express train motionless across the bridge; pigeons
who peck holes in our elegies & scatter scraps
across the grass where we share sandwiches, a blanket.
Every butterfly I've ever captured in my fist
either flew away or died. I still can't decipher

certain dissonant bars of "Trolley Song."
In truth, I've never grasped a butterfly, or tried.
But Janelle, you & the sister with whom I shared a brief,
ecstatic pyromaniac phase have much in common.
In the small miracle of our simultaneity,
we walk together, home, a burning year behind.

OF POOR J. D.

after Brecht

I, J. D. ******, confess nothing
except the crime of torturing
out of myself this confession.
I will need a fishbowl full of dirty ocean

& a volunteer to press
down on the backside of my neck.
I will need two dump trucks
full of grant money & a less

pitiful way of phrasing this:
Deluded enough to believe that within
my mother are jagged waves & coastline
folded into the shape of an intestine,

I've wasted ten years of evenings
imitating the whalesong drone
of jets as they drip hot fuel in the harbor
with a cracked-lacquer guitar

on rainy, man-made Constitution Beach.
& I, J. D. ******, after the tidal floods erase
each melody I've dragged across the sand,
will give my throat back to the ocean.

LE BONHEUR

for Agnes

The weekend Agnès Varda died, you matched me
drink for drink in my attic-kitchen—one overflowing
skull-chalice of RELAX rosé for every whiskey-
ginger I ingested. In 1965, Agnès Varda shot a film
called "Happiness," & like so many other early mornings,
that is what we drank & laughed to—near-delirium.

Told the story of trekking once from Central,
stopping for after-work cigars at Leavitt & Peirce,
then on to Harvard to hear Agnès Varda lecture.
Exhaling toxins by the Church St. exit, an Escalade
pulls up. A sunglassed, slicked, & suited chauffeur
extends a hand to abuelita Agnès, who eases

down, step by careful step, from SUV to ground.
There goes the godmother of the Nouvelle Vague,
winking at us as she passes! The story might as well end
right there (before I start fawning), with the gesture,
which is cinema, which is your arms around my neck
as you kiss me on a kitchen chair. I don't remember

if I said this two or three drinks later,
but here's what I got from *Le Bonheur*:
it's all sunflowers & Mozart until somebody breaks
a vow. For now, we're all overtime shifts, irregular gigs,
kisses between cracks in the hustle. My cinema?
It's the sunrise & half-shut eyes through which

I watch you stretch, smooth shea butter over right
leg, then left. A goodbye kiss & you're off to catch
the bus in sky-blue scrubs. Another shooting script:

You're scarved in silk against the pillowcase, streetlights
liquid through the blinds, I brush your forehead,
go chase a check across the bridge. Coming back

to find you in my sweats in front of mango peels
& an open endocrinology text, Bobby "Blue" Bland
from your facedown phone, your soft & citrus breath, your nasal
off-key hum-along, your thumb on a diagram of the adrenal gland.
Agnès was right, irising out to brightness between each scene—
before black, we fade to every color we can name.

SILENT ACTRESS OUTSIDE THE FIGHTS

Jersey City, NJ, 1923

She waits in borrowed silks & pearls
that dangle nearly to her waist,
fans herself with a fight card. She waits
outside a stadium built to be destroyed,

dry pine at the mercy of a match head.
At dusk, Luis Ángel Firpo, The Wild Bull
of the Pampas, will swing gloved knuckles
in the heat until he or The Kansas Giant collapses.

This morning she played a fortune teller
in a melodrama, in a Fort Lee billed
as Tijuana. They shrouded her eyelids
with shadow that hasn't washed off yet

& surrounded her—chiaroscuro, candlelit—
with peacock feathers & queens of hearts, sat her languid
on a Persian carpet. Remembering how she'd danced
on-screen, early summer, with a fruit basket

on her head, hating it (no Shakespearean
roles for Brazilian girls in a disposable art), she waits
for a gaucho ballad-quoting gambler at the gates
of Boyle's Thirty Acres on the Hudson.

Though soon her films will all be lost,
& though the gambler never shows,
& she goes into the fights alone, watches Firpo
pummel The Kansas Giant until he drops

to a wobbled knee against the ropes;
& though her heart aligns its accelerando
with the quickening assault, as if her fate's bound to
the bruised fists of this South American hope,

& she thrills at the knockout silently, inside
the swirl & cacophony of the crowd,
she'll catch the train back to the Ironbound,
sleep in fits &, tomorrow, like the future relies

on her performance, tell scripted fortunes
in a silent film whose every frame
will have gone missing by next war's end.

APARECIDA APPEARS THEN DISAPPEARS TO THE TUNE OF JORGE BEN JOR'S "APARECEU APARECIDA"

In the buzz of a string made of nylon or gut,
in a splinter in a moment in a single
samba-note, in the string's breath
before it sounds, in the coalescence
of the ay ay ay & the nasal
samba cry, in the choro, in Jorge Ben
Jor, in his throat & violão, is the apparition,
the outline, the sketch:
Black Madonna against a samba-black
background, blending. A casket-
shaped samba to kick through, a carnivalesque
resurrection.
        Bring me back a samba
from those concrete front-lawn summers—
Aparecida, feet bare on bottlecaps
& no grass, beats a tanned sheepskin pandeiro,
clangs its metal rings. Between lit gas
grill & ghetto blaster (it too
whispering a samba) she raises
both arms skyward. I see her through
the smoke. On a Sunday, dressed
in white. In a book of lost places.

II

CHALINO SÁNCHEZ

a sequence

[new york, 2020]

Chalino Sánchez Félix, you should be living this hour
when our borderline's barbed wire crawls vining
across a throat, when its shadows fall in spirals, & tighten.
The corrido begins like this: Declare you're
about to sing one—voy a cantar. First verse,
Glock against the smuggler's jaw. Ford Conquistador
speeding away in the second. Third & final, as silver
trumpets sway, you hear tall pines crying on their ridge.
But before all that, the corrido begins in commerce:
Barter a crime lord's tribute song for a pistol or a crucifix,
lionize a henchman for a ram's horn stuffed with twenties.
& long before all those beginnings, this:
You kill your sister's rapist at an all-night party.
You cross a border. You're fifteen, invincible & cursed.

[in la mesa prison, walking with the nun]

Mamá de la prisión,
don't mistake this for no confession:
I'm not sorry for the rapist I shot
in Culiacán, not after the shellshock

& shredded nerves he left my sister to nurse.
Mamá, waiting for your plate of mystery meat
among us convicts, barely five feet
in your black habit & dangling cross,

I have to ask: If California wouldn't keep me,
why the hell would heaven? I was a coyote
once, a crook, a pimp. I've written zero hymns
& no confessions, only drug sagas on commission

for every goon who wants his royal portrait,
his little spaghetti western tale.
Mamá de la prisión,
please sit me down in your convent-cell!

By Virgin Mary candleglow,
with the skull you adorned
in rosaries & silks our only witness,
Mamá, let me tell you this:

[I keep having this premonition]

He who takes back from the vulture
the plucked-out eyes of the narco
& points them toward the center
of the murder ballad must know

how to waltz the mineshafts
beneath Sonora, how to warm
his thorn-cut hands with doves' breath
& a thin blanket of stars

above the vineyard. He must
give back to the saguaro its honey,
to the shuttered cantina its trumpets.
Cleaning his pistol, he must hum softly.

[beverly grove]

I wanted café con leche, a little peace,
when I stopped into that coffee shop on Third
with nothing but a notepad in my Western shirt
& a corrido I half-finished months back in La Mesa.

What was I doing in that gabacho neighborhood?
Well, that's for me to know & the law to guess!
Fine, I was just at Bloomingdale's, nothing badass—
bought the wife a ruby crucifix bright as blood.

Blonde barista rapid-fired some English,
mirrored my smile. I asked for (I thought) coffee,
got some iced swill sweet as Fanta, weak as tea.
Took a corner seat & started scribbling

notes on Armando's murder—seven bullets,
messenger dove singing bad news over Sanalona,
his sons (my nephews) all fatherless & grown—
when the boss stormed out from ensconcement

to knock knuckles on my tabletop, red-jowled.
Maybe he didn't like me leaning back in snakeskin,
cowboy boots crossed on a chair, shirt unbuttoned,
or the tilt of my Tejana brim, how its shadow fell.

In that half-finished corrido, Armando, lionhearted
even through his execution at the Santa Rita hotel,
would've flipped the table, made this gringo piss himself.
Me? Parolee from La Mesa, trying not to be deported,

I bit my tongue until the song beneath it bled.
I wrapped my song in fabric the boss could never pull off,
in a language he'd never comprehend, & left.
Raising a middle finger instead of my dead.

[*I don't sing, I bark*]

One take & one take only.
The hired singer never shows & so,
unrehearsed, you bark thirteen corridos
you wrote, Guadalupe statuette glowing

red above the mixing desk.
Generations of snake eyes
rattle inside the melody—
fields of flowerless

saguaro shed thorns around
the horn chart. Your voice is what
the sawblade says to the pine knot,
what the bantam crows at the threshold

of dusk. Vamos. One take, yes,
raw—one take, yes, raw, & (clears throat):
In the city of Tijuana, a coward shot
the lionhearted Armando Sánchez . . .

[soliloquy on a car phone]

Come out! Chalino's
playing a backyard show
in Compton, a quinceañera for my neighbor's
cousin's buddy's kid. They say he shot
some wannabe onstage hitman.
They say death spotted him on the predawn
highway & hid. You seen his orchestra
at El Parral, at El Farallón,
where every show's sold out? Seen the photo
of Chalino loading the nine-
millimeter on Formica,
nonchalant? Heard his *oom-pah-pah*
blare from lowriders'
cassette decks across LA?
Compa, he's turned these cholos *country*!
You're on your way,
right? They're stringing Christmas
lights across the palm trees,
tightening a snare head with a drum key.
Accordionist & trumpet player bum a tío's
cigarettes while Chalino stalks shadows
by the fence. In a ragged whisper,
he rehearses murder ballads,
beer cold-sweating in his grip.

[to shoot a folk saint]

Friend, should you yearn to feel foolish,
we can spend the afternoon shooting

promo photos, perfecting the disaffected
grimace across six hundred & sixty-six attempts

to appear nonfuckgiving. Hard to look
hard & even harder to make the hard look

look easy. Even Chalino, loading the handgun,
concedes, in front of a lemon-honey curtain,

a shy backslash of smirk—a rip of doubt
in the icon. His eyes drift downward . . .

he's become this. On temples' ofrendas,
as template for muralist & bootlegger,

he outlasts his one life, his family curse.
The scowl—then the laugh—before flash & aperture.

[the scorpion's question mark]

Spanish tints the arachnid bitter—alacrán,
as in acridity—christens the scorpion

with a synonym for shit-talk, with gasoline & lemon,
Sinaloa coke bricks stamped with black-ink scorpions.

Who can love a sport as brutal as the one
the bootheel plays with the scorpion?

Crush him or get stung. In the hallway between
dressing room & stage, guillotine the scorpion

with one sharp footfall. & when the would-be assassin
scuffles past security, envision the scorpion,

the bootheel. Recall your cousin
on videotape, its label blank save for a scorpion

drawn in Sharpie, saying, "Everyone
in Sinaloa has a gun." 9mm CZ Scorpions,

AKs (a.k.a. goat horns), family shotgun for morning
target practice by the junkpile's sleeping scorpions.

& your failed onstage assassin, who sent him? ·
The cartel who'd stamp their cocaine with a scorpion?

A tail curls into a question—all this unknowing
& I, too, was born under the sign of the scorpion.

[santa muerte in pearl]

He sang "you left" the way the farmers sang it: "Te fuites."
    Barked it like his smuggler sagas & murder ballads, FUITES,
yes, all caps like that, & ragged as the act of leaving, fuites
    ragged in its grammar even, flipped an s & t to "fuites"
dragged it down from the hillside, keening fuites
    in the red glow of storefront studios, East LA.
      No te fuites
the mic booth until dawn, you'd cut cassette-length suites
    of true-crime corridos before your voice cracked on a "fuites,"
on that fourth dimension, memory. The way they'd whistle "fuites"
    back home in Sinaloa, & roll tobacco in a cornhusk.
      Te fuites
one morning for a show in Sinaloa, in your tinted-window pickup,
    te fuites
    after Marisela's teary "no te vayas," her week of
      premonitions. Fuites
across Tucson & Nogales, across Devil's Canyon. Fuites
    with the .45, with Santa Muerte in pearl. With rosary on
      rearview. Te fuites.

[one for adán]

What ridiculous luck to even be born.
What ridiculous luck, living long enough to sing
how your father was murdered by false policemen.
What ridiculous luck to make it through the chorus,

the next measure, next note, through the breath
before the downbeat, the "yes" that one lung says
to its twin. Adán, what, if anything, brings us together?
Arbitrary borders, a belief in curses, folk saints

who steal from the rich. Aunts, sisters, & mothers
who've suffered too damn much. A brass band
is passing. I'm back on my grandfather's shoulders
in Fall River, Mass. It's Festa do Espírito Santo,

& a sousaphone gives heartbeats to the Virgin
Mary float, cymbals clashing . . . Yes, Chalino met
his badge-flashing, sunglassed assassins outside Culiacán,
yes, your limo crashed in that same free & sovereign state,

& no, I can't match the pitch of fifteen thousand
teenagers weeping in the streets of Los Angeles,
or the mess that followed—riot gear & pellet guns,
Ford truck flipped over, in flames. But ridiculous

luck, Adán, is needed for one's own voice to adorn,
postmortem, a few romantic ballads in a locked room—
"Nadie es Eterno," "Bésame Morenita"—where two, in candlelight,
can create anything: Even a little death, even a life.

[patron saint of the swap meet]

Flea market cassettes
from Ortiz, early Sundays. Sun-faded
cassettes in suitcases, in stacks,
rows of grubby, black

& white photocopies
of Chalino loading the Glock.
Sloppy dubbed cassettes, a drunken
brass section grafted postmortem

onto *13 Mejores Éxitos*.
He lives here, between the rhinestone
prayer hands & the fortune teller's stall,
the sweet corn smoking on the grill.

[corrido under a fort myers palm]

Flea market girl handed me a flyer
for a brass band festival
going down next weekend, here
at Ortiz, featuring the "original,

world-famous Banda el Limón"—
trumpets from the fairgrounds' edge.
Later, with her flyer, I bookmarked Bolaño.
2666, "The Part About the Crimes": Juarez

factory girls go missing, baffled detectives
go insane. Chalino, could you hear that tome
thud shut? A trumpet falling through an open grave,
a brass band trapped between the crimes.

[those "mexicans for golovkin" shirts]

A bootleg of a bootleg of a bootleg.
Red screenprint on poly-cotton blends

fallen off the back of a truck.
Juan & I hawked seven boxes

outside Madison Square Garden
the night Gennadiy Golovkin

knocked out David Lemieux.
Some photos could outlive Lascaux's

charcoal, oxide, & ochre: Chalino
at the table with the cocked Tejana,

shirt unbuttoned, loading the Glock.
Some rando photoshopped that Kazakh

killer Golovkin's goofy grin onto
our narco-icon. We caught on pronto,

printed up a ream, sold Sánchez's silhouette
the same way he once sold cassettes,

on the street, then counted twenties
on the almost empty Queensbound E

where, every morning, an accordion
player wanders car to car & keens.

[new thorns, 2020]

Pull the thorns from this borderline
till barbed wire runs smooth against a palm,
till coils of concertina
fold back inside the accordion

with a sigh. Write the crime
story of this borderline & paper-plane
it into the Pacific. Let the air out of the tires
of its patrol trucks—let it fill the lungs

of protest singers. Dull the blade
of this borderline till it's only emerald
sea glass beneath the gulf. Hold
it till it dies, like a waltz,

in your arms. Robin Hood of Culiacán,
instead of bootprints on this borderline, leave a song.

III

?

APARECIDA, EARLY SUMMER

Listen: I want the shore to speak for me,
& it can't. A knot of seaweed, snarled
as a ratking, refuses to beach,
instead bobbing on the mirrored

black tide. An open sore
of rust on the overlook's bench
frames a bronze memorial for a scorpio
born two days before me, her French

name festering in metal. From the arcade,
an organ spins its arpeggios a hundred years
into the past while a half-remembered
woman by the wharf takes off her shades

& squints toward Misery Islands.
Fishing boats drift directionless
as the peeling gauze of clouds. I trust myself
less than I trust these eventual rhythms

of return, the every-morning birdsongs
from your far-off fire escape.
All I feel today is featherlight & wrong—
your single finger down my vertebrae.

DASHIELL HAMMETT

One detective lived in a country of witch hunters & bureaucrats
& wrote mysteries on harbor trash,

wet paper from shore-washed broken
bottles, & leftover film stock.

He wrote, in his office above the boardwalk,
how one detective resembled a blond Satan.

~

& how one detective hacked his name down to monosyllabics
from the lilting Greek of Charalambides,

either to sidestep tragedy's dangling axe,
or to come across American in loud speakeasies.

Hell's Kitchen, Depression, & hell's
percussion plays: the curdled bells

of highballs toasting in smoke,
cue ball's clack on the break,

one torch singer, one spilled ashtray,
one knife stuck in the body

of an upright Steinway,
one bank robber's knuckles brushing its ivory.

~

One detective lived in a country of salt breeze & profit motive
& his cough got hoarser with each world war.

Beneath the fireworks
of some hypothetical July,

one detective lived in a country
that called him, for a time, private,

patriot, purple heart—
but he knew his Marx

like the hum his typewriter made
& the seagulls above the bay,

like the black knot & labor
in his breath. One detective

walked out of his novel, he thought, forever.
Six or seven chapters later,

they found his body by the piers. "Another floater,"
said one detective, muffled between book covers.

~

& somewhere, say, in a West Virginia prison,
it's neither the detective who dies

nor the detective who survives
who goes on scrubbing toilets with a rag that thins

to paper in his fist: It's the detective
who sketched them

on inscrutable maps
in his office by the harbor

in a country of carousel music
& paranoiacs.

"Prison," one detective's
widow said, sitting

in front of the spinning
reel-to-reel on her kitchen table,

"made a thin man thinner,

~

a sick man sicker."
& though, after one detective's years of nursing

a gagged, silenced typewriter
covered in crime scene tape & spiderwebs,

they gave him the twenty-one-gun
salute, the burial at Arlington,

one detective lived in a country
of witch hunters & hitmen

& survived, for a time, to write it.

TERENCE CRAWFORD

No stories inside the heavy bag pouring its foam intestines all over the
    floor of the repurposed warehouse;
no confessions beaten out of it despite being beaten
                                      & beaten. A heavy
    bag suspended from the ceiling
never hangs completely still. Untouched for hours, watch it twitch at
    the end of its chain after the white
cylindrical lights no longer buzz & steel gates clang across the
    entrance. A few boxers walk home, gloves slung
over their shoulders, discussing slasher films. A few await an illicit
    delivery, linger out front. A few drive
to a muddy riverfront & spar bare-knuckle in moonlight.
                                          One boxer,
    thrown out of his mother's & sleeping in his Cutlass,
wakes at midnight, finds a dice game, strikes lucky, rolls a streak of
    sevens. . . . Even now, the story rattles
around my skull as if jacketed in metal: Terence Crawford, boxer,
    counting twenties, fifties, hundreds
in the front seat of his Cutlass—then a bullet piercing tinted glass.
    The rest? Promoters love to tell it
(sells tickets) & I admit, I tell myself in those weak, tremoring hours,
    how Terence Crawford, with a bullet
in his skull, drove himself to the hospital.
                                Sometimes I repeat it,
    hammering emphases: Bullet. Skull. Drove. HIMSELF.
Terence hates retelling it, resists the redemption narrative, the slick
    epiphany. He makes millions off
a fight these days, goes home to Omaha, goes fishing. . . . Slow that
    shell's rotations to half the speed of snowfall,
you'll trace its path around, & not through, cortex & tissue. Ballistics
    offers a story, but no solution.

No song in the retelling, only wind through the bones of an urban
    legend. Then the skeleton goes missing.

~

What I loved about Crawford, as I leaned over the balcony at Madison
    Square & watched him clobber
a Dominican ex-Olympian senseless, was his lack of panic, his laconic
    lean-back in the pocket, pawing,
parrying like he had eternity in the Garden, no rush to action. Then,
    the sudden southpaw shift in stance,
the strike, the sting, the straight right hand. What I loved was his
    sadist's streak & quiet arrogance.

His way of saying fuck y'all with a glance. Blood on black gloves.
    Steadily dismantling the threat.

~

As he blasted through red lights en route to the Omaha ER, what
    laundry from that Cutlass's leather interior
staunched his rushing blood—a gray, sweat-hardened wifebeater or
    sock, an improvised, tangled tourniquet
of handwraps? He's been shot at eight times since, his estimate.
                              A chorus:
    These streets are—this sport is—war
& what's war resolved? Nothing, yuh?
                      A chorus:—with Cutlass,
    laundry, & blood—for Terence Crawford's
sniper-steady dice & uppercuts, hitting lucky sevens & solar plexuses as
    if he'll never miss, has never missed before.

BOSSA NOVA WAS INVENTED IN A BATHROOM

The samba would no longer shower
>   (João Gilberto spoke only in whispers)

He hid behind the drawn curtains of the samba
>   (Two chords droning, the samba's silk unraveled)

He holed up in his sister's flat in Diamantina
>   (He paid his rent in tangerines)

He was, like the green-eyed monastery wolves, nocturnal
>   (All to echo the washerwomen's rhythm at the river)

The piled-up laundry was a sculpture of Medusa
>   (Remembering washboards, silks, & wicker)

His bim boms ping-ponged off brittle, porcelain hexagons
>   (Drain flies buzz across nasal harmonics)

The balladeer must go DOWN to THE RIVER ad infinitum
>   (A faucet is no less a river than a river)

TIM MAIA IN MIAMI, 1963

Stoned & sandaled, with the Black Power afro & bad-toothed grin,
    indecipherable to Everglade bohemians
who buy their herb from him—even his given name, Sebastião,
    registers only as a nasal honk & two soft lisps.
So they call him *Tim* . . .
Brazil, his inscrutable origin, is still just tourism & rainforest to
        Americans, Black Orpheus
& Carmen Miranda's banana headdress. No one's sure how he got
    here, to Florida's nadir, though his
alibi is "student" & he's been singing baritone in a doo-wop quartet.
    This was before The Boatlift, before Castro emptied
his prisons on the shore; before Spanglish threaded every salt breeze &
    before they realized South Beach was sinking into the sea.
Before das kapital of Latin America's young capital was weighed in
    cocaine metrics—no eight-balls yet, no kilos. & plenty
of time, still, until Tim brings Soul to Brazil, becomes a homegrown
    Otis Redding of the open-air discotheque, re-
makes those early doo-wop demos with cosmic-samba beats; achieves,
    as it's called in pop music, immortality.
No—it's September '63, & the immortal's still a bum. They still don't
    know what the fuck he's saying, these floral-
shirted collegians, every vowel turning to wet sand in his jowls, every
    consonant whistling through crooked teeth,
& even when he laughs, throaty, throwing his head back, a gospel
    choir trying to kick out of his chest, the joke's as unplaceable
as his accent.
        But soon—they're not sure why—they're laughing too, &
    soon he's partying among them, parting the beaded curtains
of some Art Deco apartment—Beat poets on the bookshelves, endless
    bottles of absinthe & gin. He stays

till morning, scribbling broken English love lyrics on a new bohemian
    girlfriend's skin. "I've slept in the street," he'll sing, ten
years later. Tonight, however, he stays awake, holding this strange girl
    close, so close that the ink rubs against him, then away.

~

Late autumn, sleepless again, in Dade County prison, acting the part
    of the hapless white-sand romantic, singing
bossa nova through the bars, diverting, for a moment, the guard's
    attention from a tin tobacco spit-cup,
he awaits deportation. But why this sentence? The kid's no capo, no
    don, no Scarface, no Escobar.

One hundred-odd miles from the Bay of Pigs & what goes on? An
    unknown soul singer gets busted smoking blunts in a stolen car,
then, for a few nights, is locked up. A minor crime, innocuous, even;
    pitiful by Vice City standards, no deed of a kingpin.
But let me print this little legend:
                                One year later, Brazil falls to
    military dictatorship. I like to imagine
Tim never flinches under its iron fist, even as the cineastes, the poets,
    Caetano, Gilberto, his brethren,
are exiled, jailed, or shot—the lucky ones slip to London, sculpting
    torch-songs out of fog. I like to picture Tim,
the scoundrel, *O Malandro* of neverending street-songs, deported back
    to the corner, throwing the shaved dice
of discontent, acting out the gnarled, sly resistance of an exile in
    reverse. Protected by his so-called only vice:
"I don't drink, I don't smoke, I don't snort, I don't cheat . . .
                                        but I lie."

APARECIDA WITH A NEEDLE IN HER ARM

Lately, I've been seeing
the prayer hands of cheap pendants
& RIP tattoos come to life
then swell beyond life-size
like the tender, jeweled,
& severed fists of giants—
though these prayer hands
are off-brand, the knockoff steel
of turn-your-lobes-green earrings,
they too are holy, the gleam of Chet
Baker's syringe as it hovers above
the garbage can & he glides
into the mic booth, silver trumpet
over one suspendered, white teed
shoulder, to sing, vibrato-free,
in praise of the way he walks: winged,
clumsy, weightless, loved—how lately
my thoughts are running on as if I could fit
every not-yet-forgotten name of my fallen
into a single comma-savaged sentence;
how even a rest in peace or power tattoo
muraling a mourner's arm is filled
with the threat of its own infection
long after—& before—the needle
hovers above a clean & naked skin

SIGHTING: ON THE BEACH WITH BRYSON

Though his name is distant, anglicized & inherited from a drunk,
    runaway uncle existing only in shredded
Polaroids, & though he, until late adolescence, lived as a shadow
    against ghetto blocks my mother shunned & shepherded
me away from, though our time together consisted only of that one
    southwest Florida summer, Bryson's my blood.

His past's less narrative than question, less question than mumbled
    ellipsis: Xbox, sugar cereal, blasting rap-metal with buddies
back in New Bedford, Mass, most, I guessed, dead. His mother dead,
    for a fact—trash mom,
the family whispers went: how she'd send him out for pain pills on the
    corner, aged ten. . . . Enough trauma—

it's August, Fort Myers Beach. Both of us carless, walking—me
    sixteen & clueless, he twenty-three & just released—
with wax-wrapped egg salad sandwiches (dodging divebombing
    seagulls) & mismatched physiques:
malnourished teenage bantamweight beside hardened barbell vet.
    His fade fresh-clipped, my ponytail slicked; his blinding

silver cross in the sun. Already heat exhaustion sweat. Already
    directionless. "We should've
        brought *something*,"
Bryson said, "at least a football."
                "Or a book!" I added. He looked at
    me like I'd suggested dipping

our sandwiches in the sand. No entertainment, then, but the
    water—more threat than anything,

both of us inept swimmers—where we'd wade-walk, watch for
     bikinis. I wonder how they typecast us, those Gulf
Coast girls we'd eyefuck—indiscreetly pointing with our noses to
     signal the presence of a MILF

or bombshell in the water—did they see two young Latin lovermen,
     or Criminals #5 & #6? Did they picture
me or him mid-kiss with the starlet in a sunset dissolve, or getting
     shot in a botched pawnshop stick-up?
In reality, no acknowledgment—no re-flirtation, or disgust towards
     us—& if not for dehydration,

I might have forgotten I existed; our conversation was, amid the
     ogling, languid & flickering as a hallucination.

Think: There must have been something important, some prison
     story or street knowledge my cousin imparted
to make me realize lockup was not the Iceberg Slim Writers' Colony
     & pulling a gun was not performance art.

That maybe Bryson, as he floated up to his neck, convinced me to
     stop shoplifting from the Walmart
near our aunt's one-story where we both lived out that summer—
     that ghost-suburb of empty swimming
pools & FOR SALE signs, of every-evening thunderstorms. But I
     remember nothing except those girls in the distance

& how shameless we were, Mexico behind us. Past the horizon,
     aimless & infinite August. Pushing against
the current towards the shore, seeing those three teen girls, their
     long braids & hypnotic frisbee, spinning, spinning. . . .

He's law-abiding now, I heard. Scrapes by on hard labor, graveyard
     shift. Met a backwater princess

on the internet, moved out west. Married, with pit bull, he blames
    his pitiful wages on more-recent immigrants.
But I'll never forget three girls laughing in salt breeze, their coral &
    teal bikinis, the infinite spin

of their frisbee. How one girl's eyes, brown & owl-sized, though they
    never met mine, looked through me. & then
my cousin's hand on my shoulder, his loaded question towards the
    punchline: "Know what those girls look like?"
"What, Bryson?"
           "Jail time."

AMEN WAS A BANTAMWEIGHT

he strolled into the gym
after a year away & said
he'd seen some shit we couldn't fathom
done some shit he'd take to his grave

But Amen liked to talk a lot
said he once knocked out Pacquiao
over a parking spot
pow! pow!
yeah, Amen had imagination
& a theme song that went:

"You better say amen
cross yourself or something
better say amen
You better say amen
when you see me coming
better say amen"

Said he spent the spring in Mexico
boxing bare-knuckle
in Quintana Roo sunshine
in makeshift, open-air casinos
between corrido singers & cockfights

Amen was on a winning streak
till he woke up drunk cuddling a married chica
ay!
killed the husband in a kitchen fistfight
then crossed the border whistling:

"You better say amen
when you see me coming
better say amen"

Said her husband was some cartel goon
connected in the States
with mad cousins prowling town
so Amen kept a loaded Magnum
in his gym bag under tangled handwraps

One day, from the locker room
everybody in the building

heard a thunderfucking
BOOM
& there's Amen in a piss-soaked jockstrap
on the floor, whispering:

"You better say amen
when you see me coming
better say amen."

He claims it was intentional
he fired off a shot
to hype himself up ("I'm TOO raw")
you could hear his myth asphyxiating
hairlines in his tenor, cracking

That afternoon he sparred a high school kid
the rookie lit him up, split his lip
& made him quit
That was the last I saw of Amen
but every now & then I sing:

You better say amen
when you see me coming
better say amen.

APARECIDA A YEAR AFTER THE FACT

Even when I wasn't searching I was searching: walking the grease-
    stained sidewalks of storefront auto garages,
envisioning holograms in the oil pools, high harmonies in the
    pneumatic drills. & though I witnessed countless
sixty mile-per-hour near-misses around the blind curve (a flight
    attendant's silhouette & wheeled luggage
frozen between headlights & median, then the brake screech, the
    Civic's lingering exhaust, her ringing curses)
no one died, at least not on my street, overlooking Boston Casket
    Co., its taunting marquee at the intersection.

Though I've hit heavy bags beside young men with teardrops
    tattooed below their eyes, I haven't murdered,
or even cried. A year's gone by, Aparecida—arid, incessant—in the
    slow burn of cornerstore incense,
the rotten mango smell of its ash.
                          Though I've worked long hours
    in a brutalist building, my small, concrete
purgatory & all summer, watched wrecking crews, from my window,
    knock other buildings down, leaving gashes
across the city's face, I've spent my breaks in a projectionist's booth-
    turned-meditation chamber lit with plastic,
glow-in-the-dark stars & a holographic poster of deep space. I'm not
    quite praying. In a town rebuilt by Catholic racketeers,
where they've paved & repaved over these visions, Aparecida,
    you're the oil pool & teardrop. You're the exhaust.

ON FUTURE RHYMING "FUCK YOU" WITH "FUCK YOU" FOUR TIMES IN A ROW DURING "RENT MONEY"

I want you to hear this and be like, "Man, he gave us all of him. He let everything out."

—*Future*

There's more church in a one-note drone on my collaborator's organ-
simulation software than I've seen the inside of this year. Origin

stories bore me to tears, but let's say fuck it & start back in the barrio:
Summers, I'd shoot hoops in a fútbol-only barrio,

have languid, lonely shootarounds at caged-in Constitution Beach,
rapping along to my boombox, going silent on every motherfucker
    or bitch

for fear of retribution. God was still listening then. I stayed close to
    sunstroke,
shooting endless threes, my release point smoothed to butter. Never
    had a sweeter stroke

& no one around to see it. Well, there was the occasional five-on-five
among full-grown men, but my jump shots all got swatted. Wasn't
    even five

feet tall then, weighed less than a sweat-soaked towel thrown over a
    park bench.
What I loved, way more than full-court—with its trash talk, thrown
    elbows, constant bench-

riding, & Beckett-lengths of waiting to sub in—& even more than
    solitude, were shootarounds
in tandem, trio, quartet. Once a young Matheus came around,

a Matheus I'd never met, would never see again. Brazilian, lanky, braids
hanging past his neck, I remember watching him leap to grab the
long, white, braided

x-stitch of the net (it glowed pristine, as if City Parks, at dawn, had
changed it); I rem-
ember him pulling & pulling until it ripped from the rim

& how he seemed to do it for no reason.
Everything, then, happened for a reason.

The rhythm of dribble/brick/pavement/rim paced
the conversation—between the ball's bright pings, or over a
bounce pass,

we'd say our piece. Matheus dished a rumor about a Boston
Latin soccer star, why he retired aged sixteen: "Bro, he busted

inside his girl without a condiment. Now he's got a sex disease."
Just as likely: the dizzy

spells of a surprise first trimester, the high school winger quitting,
picking up full-time
shifts at a Revere Beach roast beef stand. Or maybe just
running. Time

is money, Heidegger, I believe, wrote. Your baby mama fucks me
better when the rent's due,
Future rapped, & do I believe them dudes?

Truth be told, I slipped a hundred and two fifties into a single
mother's hand-
bag once, aged twenty, told her "Baby, get your braids done." She
just handed

back the cash, closed my fist &, patting it, whispered, "Keep it, boy.
     Your rent's due."
The fantasy & its own undoing:

that silver might drip from a neck bitten or a back clawed hard
     enough. For just one faux-sure
sentence, let me envision what happened to varsity winger & wifey,
     fucking away one future

as they improvised another; let me envision the fruit of their
     improvisation full-
grown now, throwing elbows in a full-

court game of beachfront five-on-five, banging on the worn-paint
     asphalt. The same court
where I once shot jumpers with switchblade-thin Marselly & her
     older cousin Courtney,

both shrinkwrapped in Brazilian jeans, their gold hoop earrings
     untouchable & distant
as the rim. A drizzling Monday, seagulls in the distance,

the matching cousins' snapping gum, their *mierda*s every time
     they missed.
They asked me why I didn't swear, & in what today I might consider
     a misstep, some mystic

shit, or simply a "missed shot," I told them I'd made a contract
     with God.
Nowadays, I can't get through a prayer without a few fucks for
     emphasis, just ask God.

Nowadays, I'm convinced any word that keeps repeating
& repeating is a prayer. Like when Future finds an end-line fuck you
     & repeats it

till it's mantra.

So, broken courtside boombox, go on whispering
through your landfill *yes yes y'all & you don't stop.*
& Future, autotuned, on cough syrup, on loop, rhyming fuck you
with fuck you till eternity: don't stop.

IV

GATO BARBIERI
a sequence

"The jazz people, they don't consider me a jazz musician. If I am Latin, they don't consider me Latin. So I am here in the middle. It's a good thing, you know why? Because they say, 'What do you play?' I say, 'I play my music: Gato Barbieri'."

[first tango]

The man in the dusk-colored glasses
haunts my neighborhood with his sax.

On a street corner better described
as an absence, he harmonizes

with the car alarms & howling strays.
Throw a dollar in his open case

& watch it fall forever, as if through
a night sodden with every other blue-

black night that was, or might have been.
They say before the cars & even

before the feral dogs & avenues,
before any of the above was imaginable,

he'd make a ram's horn cry, coax a low
whistle from the brittle throat of a crow.

They say, when it was just the night & him,
he taught the night what lonely meant.

[sighting: saxman at 125th]

Seen Gato on the platform—
what you mean he's dead & gone?!

Seen him in the station with his sax,
125th in midday dregs—deadass.

Crumple up his obit from the *Times*
& toss it, let it stoke a track fire

for all I care, Gato's out here
honking like he escaped an asylum

where inmates get tortured
three times a minute with foghorn

blare. It's Gato, man, it's him. Ideas
snake out from under his smuggler's

fedora. Glasses the color of dusk
in a deserted city on a tilted sphere

warmed only by a far-off torment of flares.
This subway's hot as hades & Gato's

screeching *Caliente!* as if to smother
its fires with a flurry of grace notes

& steal a little stillness from the air.

[the man in the dusk-colored glasses on authenticity]

They often mistake me for the Argentine.
It doesn't bother me. I've been mistaken

for worse: a bugler beheaded in a cavalry charge,
a punk who snaps the strings of lyres

for laughs. A common misconception:
I'm married to the Muse. Fact is, we haven't

seen each other since Athens, that disastrous
bacchanal. Bad grapes & alimony ever after.

The Catholics tell me all books, crap or classics,
are authored by the Holy Spirit. I'm more sparrow

than theologian so, good or ill, I make no claims
on Spirit. But I know all songs—since the first vein

hummed with its blue debut of blood—clamor
& scrape toward the same canopy of stars.

Admittedly, I may have once possessed
the body & blood of the Argentine, that sax-

man known as Gato B., for that brief flicker
colloquially known as a lifespan. No matter.

A voice on a radio breaks like bread
as I flee a city swamped with light. Jazz is dead,

the static says, & a muddy shovel clatters a sly
rhythm in my trunk that proves otherwise.

[pasar mi vida cantando]

All day screeching through this instrument
till the throat's raw & the only reward
is the desire to screech no more.
I thought my time would be best spent

this way, in the daylight between grace notes,
tongue against a splintered reed, air bent
into the shape of metal after a car wreck.
I thought trouble would leave me like a parasite

after the last antibiotic, but I know better now.
Tonight, my record spins in a mirrored discotheque
where I teach a smuggler's mistress card tricks
& pull a conman's brim across my brow.

[gato b. on antarctic science]

Easier to craft some elaborate comparison
than to simply admit you're alone.
Years ago, in a hotel whose moisture-savaged
ceiling is indistinguishable from the one

I talk to tonight, I caught the last half
of a late-night film about Antarctic scientists,
one of whom was possessed by shapeshifting evil—
or maybe they all were, it was hard to tell—

but either way, it ended in frostbite & flames.
I've never ventured to the dagger blade that twists
my country's south toward the Antarctic
but, for decades on the road, I felt much the same,

isolated in my arcane discipline. Blue ice & red flares
throwing on everything a light only I could see.
This, I said to myself, or to the muted screen,
is *you*, these researchers playing poker in flannel underwear

knowing the shapeshifter will soon possess them.
In hotel mirrors, I used to see a reflection
of a man so *like* me that I would have been forgiven
for never giving him a second glance.

But I stared him down, like a boxer at a weigh-in,
waited for him to flinch, & when he did, I felt a twinge
the likes of which I've only felt at the knifepoint
of a melody when it scrapes upwards, unbroken, from throat

to night sky. He was the lamplight & cry inside the sax.
Not the cry—its residue & wreak. & from that moment,
I knew only two things could ever kill me: Fire, or him.
The mirror spiderwebbed, the both of us ash.

[from a waterfront bar, watching the jet skis]

I'm from Argentina, not Galilee,
but tonight I watch two men walk on the water.
Minor miracles suffice for me,
even the lamplit glint I'd forgotten

on the blue until two distant figures'
motorized, ecstatic back & forth
lent me a pair of beginner's
eyes so I could watch the harborfront

once more in bafflement & wonder.
What could you add, what could I
add to a stilled wave's whisper? Nada,
nada. Regardless, take this horn & try.

[the dirty war as seen through dusk-colored glasses]

Here I am with a fraction of a prophet's tongue
& a rusted tenor, trying to make a song

from the same shrapnel that's rendered four thousand
years of holy men speechless or insane.

Alone by the ocean with a rusted horn, one can't be
sure of the difference between idea & salt spray, melody

& other winged miseries. I watch a lone wasp
burrow in sand & wish I could listen close

enough to hear an electric current sing
through a single synapse, blood keen

through latticework in blue. Who'd need music,
then? I could toss this instrument to tidewrack,

let it make a home among the bent metal
of a minor shipwreck, let

beach roses weave through absences where its keys
once opened & closed. I come from a country

where the railroad reaches the end of the world:
All I know for sure is the way its iron tracks curve

into a question. Back home, inside the basilica,
masked men kidnap a diplomat and carve an infinity

sign into his windpipe. Or so goes the legend.
Here I am at the edge of a strange continent

with nothing but a rusted horn, a list of questions
longer than a prophet's scroll, & two working lungs,

having escaped, once more, the eye of the storm.
My name is Gato Barbieri. This is my war report.

[the man in the dusk-colored glasses on gato b.]

Everywhere I go, I take the borderline with me.
& so for luck, & because I must, I cross myself
each morning. Across the white of a saint's eye,

I trace red latticework that leads me,
maplike, to the scorched outskirts of the self,
& even there I can't find a better definition of "I"

than the sound a vowel makes when held. Mi,
re, do—don't matter. Hold these sounds to be self-
replicant. Hold them till the breath expires. I

once missed a woman so madly that my
sax & I scavenged unnamable notes. Note to self:
No G-sharp could reach her. I needed an H, an I.

I needed a breath strong enough to dissolve me,
a mezcal to submerge the worm of my self,
a sad milonga at midnight that could cry (ay ay)

a whole nightclub to sleep—a seedy, seamy
hole-in-the-wall trimmed with cellophane
garland & flowers that will never die. I

once loved a woman with such alarming sanity (sue me)
that, just to drape her in cashmere & Hermès, I pressed myself
into kitsch-disco records by the million, & spun. I

pity those who hear in every pulse a death-march. Me,
I no longer fear disco, or the human heart, those self-
replicating, metronomic knells of the inevitable. I

alone am wild enough to frighten me.
Between myself & death I place Gato Barbieri.

[sundress & nail]

Sound is air that's pushed around
or coaxed or pulled or just allowed
to wander on volition, to billow
through your sundress hanging on a nail.

From the stairway, a spoon's faint chime
against coffee cup ceramic
echoes in my chest like a church bell.
Here, upstairs, your sundress on a nail,

floral & silk against blank brick,
rustles like windchimes with their throats slit,
makes a music of its own denial,
a song where sundress & nail

give refuge to two mute sparrows. No,
our music is not this air, not this hollowed-
out space through which all freefalls.
This sundress hanging on a nail

is not the body you once gave it
when you came to it salt-wet & naked,
parting the beaded curtain, Michelle,
taking down your sundress from a nail.

[shadow & boxer]

My friend the heavyweight equates boxing & jazz:
The better they are, the less they're understood.
So if I sing you this story in code
& cryptolect, if I twist the angel's trumpet blast

into a bronze & molten sculpture of my home
country with its orbital bone caved in,
don't blame me: I'm just an instrument
holding an instrument through which a spume

of hawk's breath drifts. Sound is wind & wind
was howling afterhours against the bar's
smoked glass. Boxing & jazz: the better they are,
the less motherfuckers appreciate them,

said the gold-chained heavyweight
who'd come backstage to philosophize
& hang. We both went silent while
he twisted his chain into a figure eight

& his gaze drew ellipses. In lieu of speech,
I followed him out a black backdoor
(a door I'd always assumed led nowhere)
into an absence masquerading as a street.

A shadow that might have been my own
scraped a metal rake across pavement-
colored emptiness. The heavyweight was gone.
Dawn was breaking. Bent into a question,

the shadow hummed a two-note, inscrutable hymn
I've never dared capture on my instrument,
though even now I remember it the way a calm
blue water remembers an open palm.

[the man in the dusk-colored glasses on obscurity]

For years, I lived for the SECRET
buzzing around my skull,
a sound that didn't meet—
that, in fact, completely failed—

the first requirement of sound,
since no one else could hear it.
Still, I carried it in the frailest
cradle imaginable, shrouded

only by a thin blanket of bone.
For years, I left the SECRET prone
to blotting itself out in a bar brawl
(the skull cracked, leaking) or four-

story fall—I was willing to gamble.
If I died, I wanted the SECRET
dead, too, in my arms: a heartsick
bride in a lachrymose tango.

Sometimes, in the backhoe
or blackbird, I still catch echoes
of what I lived for once, & smile. But the SECRET,
now, is only sound. I no longer hear it.

[last tango]

To sing & not waver in
this brief air we're given:
to carry a string of bells
past the storm wind-

battered seawall,
calmly, in this brief squall
between long twin nothings
of will be & was,

with insane faith
in the winged shadow
growing closer who takes
you by the throat

& dares you to sing
with a prophet's lung

NOTES

The opening epigraphs come from John Edgar Wideman's *Fanon* and Ludwig Wittgenstein's "On Certainty."

"On the Beach at Night with Pete" paraphrases a lyric from "Fisherman" by The Congos, cited in the text.

"Drunk with the Mermaid" flips a line from Hart Crane's "Voyages": "The bottom of the sea is cruel."

"Beach Rose" is after Eugenio Montale's "[portami il girasole . . .]" and Tupac Shakur's "The Rose That Grew from Concrete."

"Of Poor J. D." is after Bertolt Brecht's "Of Poor B.B."

"New York, 2020" owes a debt of gratitude to William Wordsworth's "London, 1802."

"I Keep Having This Premonition" owes a debt of gratitude to Anna Akhmatova's "Boris Pasternak."

"I Don't Sing, I Bark" translates (freely) a lyric from Chalino Sánchez's "Armando Sánchez" ("en la ciudad de Tijuana, señores, esto pasó / murió un hombre de valor, un cobarde lo mató").

"Dashiell Hammett" borrows briefly from Hammett's *The Maltese Falcon:* (". . . resembled a blonde Satan") and Lillian Hellman's essay "Dashiell Hammett: A Memoir" (". . . made a thin man thinner, a sick man sicker").

"Terence Crawford" owes a debt of gratitude to Mark Kriegel's article "The Education of Terence Crawford."

"Tim Maia in Miami, 1963"—translates a lyric from Tim Maia's "Bom Senso" (". . . I've slept in the street").

"On Future Rhyming 'Fuck You' with 'Fuck You' Four Times in a Row During 'Rent Money'" takes its epigraph from Future's interview with Zane Lowe's World Record program on Beats 1 Radio. The poem also contais a quoted lyric from Future's "Rent Money" ("your baby mama fucks me better when the rent's due"), cited in the text.

On the title page to "Gato Babieri: A Sequence," the epigraph comes from Barbieri's *New York Times* obituary.

The image of Gato Barbieri on the title page is titled "Durante la pausa in studio di registrazione con Gato Barbieri," and the photograph was taken by Giuseppe Pino.

"Shadow & Boxer" flips a quote from George Foreman: "Boxing is like jazz. The better it is, the less people appreciate it."

"Last Tango" owes a debt of gratitude to José Luís Mendonça's "Pode ser que o mundo acabe na semana que vem."

And massive respect for their overarching, unquantifiable influence on this book, to Aimé Césaire, Jay Wright, and Sterling A. Brown.

ACKNOWLEDGMENTS:

9x5 (anthology, Only Human Press, 2022): "The Voice of Hercules," "Bossa Nova Was Invented in a Bathroom," "Drunk with the Mermaid," "On Future Rhyming 'Fuck You' with 'Fuck You' Four Times in a Row During 'Rent Money'," "*Le Bonheur*," "New York, 2020," "Beverly Grove," "One for Adán," and "Those 'Mexicans for Golovkin' Shirts"

$: Poetry Is Currency: "Amen Was a Bantamweight"

The Adroit Journal: "Beverly Grove"

American Chordata: "Aparecida with a Needle in Her Arm"

Apogee: "Tim Maia in Miami, 1963"

The Cincinnati Review: "Those 'Mexicans for Golovkin' Shirts"

Diode: "Aparecida, Early Spring," "Aparecida, Early Summer"

FreezeRay: "*Le Bonheur*," "Bossa Nova Was Invented in a Bathroom"

Invisible City: "Drunk with the Mermaid"

the minnesota review: "New York, 2020"

Narrative: "On Future Rhyming 'Fuck You' with 'Fuck You' Four Times in a Row During 'Rent Money'"

Ninth Letter: "The Voice of Hercules"

Palette Poetry: "The Man in the Dusk-Colored Glasses on Gato B."

Salamander: "One for Adán," "Corrido Under a Fort Myers Palm," "New Thorns, 2020"

Salt Hill: "First Tango"

Sepia: "Sundress & Nail"

Witness: "I Don't Sing, I Bark"

The Worcester Review: "Gato B. on Antarctic Science," "From a Water-front Bar, Watching the Jet Skis"

Words & Sports Quarterly: "Terence Crawford"

THANKS

Every moment in which we don't get run over by a bus is an act of grace. To think that I've been able to string together enough of such moments to write this book leaves me in a state of bafflement and wonder. I owe it all to the Father, the Son, the Holy Spirit, through whom all things are possible, through whom all things are made, and through whom I have been blessed with incredible elders, parents, siblings, and friends. When I'm hitting the right notes, it's not me singing, it's all of them singing through me. The wrong notes (which are merely the whimperings of the ego) are all mine.

And here at the end, let me light a candle for my cousin Scott: Wish you were here to see this.

The Scorpion's Question Mark by J. D. Debris
Winner of the 2022 Donald Justice Poetry Prize,
selected by Cornelius Eady

Given by Liza Katz Duncan
Winner of the 2022 Rising Writer Prize in Poetry,
selected by Donika Kelly

Ishmael Mask by Charles Kell

Origami Dogs: Stories by Noley Reid

Taking to Water by Jennifer Conlon
Winner of the 2022 Autumn House Poetry Prize,
selected by Carl Phillips

Discordant by Richard Hamilton
Winner of the 2022 CAAPP Book Prize,
selected by Evie Shockley

The Neorealist in Winter: Stories by Salvatore Pane
Winner of the 2022 Autumn House Fiction Prize,
selected by Venita Blackburn

Otherwise: Essays by Julie Marie Wade
Winner of the 2022 Autumn House Nonfiction Prize,
selected by Lia Purpura

For our full catalog please visit: http://www.autumnhouse.org